endorsements

"I would recommend this book for anyone, as it provides solutions for many of life's difficult problems."
—Rev. Earnie Dorey, Lone Butte, B.C.

"In *From Fear to Freedom,* Bev Brown writes on becoming free from emotional bondage with great insight and clarity. I believe this work is destined to become a great soul-winning tool for the Lord Jesus Christ. If you are longing for freedom from condemnation, if you are longing to know the Father's love, if you are longing to be able to give love, then this book will lead you on the pathway of that discovery. This is a timely book for such a hurting and troubled world as ours."
—Rev. Mary Gharzouzi, Toronto, Ontario

from
fear
to
freedom

BEVERLEY BROWN

from fear to freedom

My Journey to Wholeness Through Faith in Jesus Christ

Pleasant Word

A Division of WINEPRESS PUBLISHING

Pleasant Word (a division of WinePress Publishing, PO Box 428, Enumclaw, WA 98022) functions only as book publisher. As such, the ultimate design, content, editorial accuracy, and views expressed or implied in this work are those of the author.

Unless otherwise indicated, all Scriptures are taken from the New American Standard Bible, © 1960, 1963, 1968, 1971, 1972, 1973, 1975, 1977 by The Lockman Foundation. Used by permission.

The names of all the people who are introduced in the first chapter have been changed to fictional names, to protect their privacy.

ISBN 13: 978-1-4141-0736-3
ISBN 10: 1-4141-0736-6
Library of Congress Catalog Card Number: 2006903417

table of contents

CHAPTER 1

The circle

"The fear of man brings a snare."

—Prov. 29:25a

That *was* good!" exclaimed Mr. Nickel. He came up to me, rubbing his hands together, his eyes beaming. I had just played a piano piece I had written for his master class. Seated in front of me was a young fellow by the name of Neal. He turned around and whispered, "That was *really good!*"

"How long did it take you to write?" asked Mr. Nickel.

"Forever!" I answered. Everyone laughed.

"Have you written it out?" he wanted to know.

"I have, but I lost it," I replied.

I heard a groan from the row behind me. It was Stephen, a student of Mr. Nickel's. It was he who had suggested I play my piece for the class. He sounded so disappointed. How could I have lost it? Mr. Nickel asked a few more questions, for he had never met me before and his curiosity had been aroused.

"What are you doing?" he asked.

I evaded his question as best I could. After all, how could I say that I spent my time reading anatomy books and T. S. Eliot, teaching a small class of piano students, and composing here at the Conservatory without permission? So after a few awkward answers that I hoped had satisfied him, the class continued.

Others got up to play while Mr. Nickel coached them. They were all studying piano here at the Victoria Conservatory of Music. Most had chosen music as their career and would become piano teachers, performers, adjudicators, and examiners. *Is this ever an exciting place!* I thought, as I gazed at the elegant chandeliers that hung from the ceiling. The building itself was a splendid old castle built in the 1800s, and this room had been the living room. Classical music blended in beautifully with this setting.

Among Mr. Nickel's numerous students present in this class were Suzanne and Keith. I had met them both several weeks earlier, when they and Stephen had listened with interest to my composition. Suzanne got up to play a Chopin etude. Afterwards, Mr. Nickel sat down and demonstrated how she must *reach* for those high notes. Everyone was so amiable. After the class, she joked with me about how nervous I had been.

"You have exactly the same symptoms as I do when I'm nervous!" she laughed. "My hands shake and my foot on the pedal feels like it's going into the floor!"

"You played your piece really well!" exclaimed Stephen, coming up to us. "Nice clean octaves, not too much pedal. And everyone was so quiet! Usually everyone's whispering and talking."

I felt I had been unusually honored.

Later that evening, Neal shared with me how he was taking a composition class as one of his courses at university. He was in his first year of a four-year music program at the University of Victoria.

Mr. Nickel had a few more words with me as well.

"Where are you from?" he asked, for I was a new-comer to Victoria.

"Saskatoon," I replied.

"Wow, that's a long way from here. How old are you?" he wanted to know.

"Twenty-one."

He looked a little shocked. I definitely didn't look twenty-one. Then he started to discuss my composing. He tried to persuade me to take composition lessons, suggesting two well-known composition teachers in the city.

"They're both very nice," he assured me. He then discussed the prospect of teaching me piano, even going so far as to offer to teach me for free. I took him up on it for a short while. Meanwhile I continued to go to the Conservatory because I needed a place to compose, not owning a piano for the time being, and I also found the environment stimulating.

Suzanne soon became my best friend. Her interest in music, her sense of humor, and her acceptance of people made her a very enjoyable person. I both hoped and believed that Suzanne and I would be lifelong friends.

Then there was Stephen. He was a wonderful person—warm, friendly, and extremely bright. After just one year of piano lessons, he was playing difficult pieces such as Beethoven's *Moonlight Sonata* and *The Carnival* by Robert Schumann! The average person would need to study piano for years before attempting such pieces. But Stephen was anything but average. Everybody liked him. He also had a delightful sense of humor. I remember one time I came to the Conservatory, carrying a medical book on the brain. Immediately he noticed it and asked, "Does it say where you can buy one?"

Before long, Stephen offered to play a few of my pieces in the Canadian Composers' Class in the festival. I loved the idea. After all, Stephen was an outstanding pianist. Would it not give me considerable prestige to have him play them?

Many talented and dedicated musicians were studying here. Charles, a student of Mr. Nickel's, had placed second in the Canadian National Competition. Teresa, also studying with Mr. Nickel, had been a top student at the university in her hometown. I overheard someone saying how hard it must be for Teresa to go from being at the top to being at the bottom. But that's how it was in Victoria. (Actually, Teresa was far from being at the bottom; she was very gifted and was doing very well in her piano studies.)

Also studying were several girls from Hong Kong. Lori, from Calgary, was in her third year of a four-year music program at the University of Victoria. Due to personal and emotional problems, however, she was unable to complete the school year. Nonetheless, she continued private piano instruction from Mr. Nickel's wife, also an excellent piano teacher and pianist. Jack, a very fine cello student, was also pursuing a career in music here at the Victoria Conservatory of Music. I remember working on a duet for piano and violin and needing a string player – any kind of string player – to try out the violin part with me. Teresa went off to find one. Before I knew it, up three flights of stairs came Jack with his cello, into the studio where I was composing!

Stephen, Keith, and Suzanne were all working hard. Both Stephen and Keith put in four two-hour practice sessions at the piano—daily.

"Boy, when I go to do the last session, after having done six hours already, I think, *two more hours!*" Keith admitted one night. His schedule took quite a toll on him. Then he and Suzanne compared what time they each got up in the morning. Keith got up at 6:00 A.M. and started his two-mile bike ride to the Conservatory. Suzanne got up slightly later.

"But we both get to the Castle at the same time," Suzanne pointed out. Keith looked a bit defeated.

"The advantages of living close to the Castle!" she laughed, for she lived only three blocks away.

I grew to like Keith.

"You're really some composer," he said to me after an evening of practicing in a studio next to mine.

"You're going to be really famous!" Lori piped up.

"Leave me in your will," Keith insisted. He came up with my nickname "composer-in-residence" because I went there every evening to compose without fail. I loved it.

But I was getting nervous. The practice rooms were supposed to be for students only. I wasn't a student. What if, eventually, regulations were enforced and I were not allowed to use the facilities any longer? In my apprehensiveness, I started dedicating my pieces to certain people in the circle, Stephen first, then Suzanne. I had plans for several more such dedications, all with the hope of binding them to me, of creating an obligation on their part so that they wouldn't take away from me the privilege of being among them.

But far from trying to exclude me, they sought to include me in things they were doing.

"Why don't you play one of your pieces for the Musical Arts Club?" suggested Keith. "They would be very grateful."

Though I didn't take him up on it, I was invited to the Musical Arts Christmas party and to a performance of Handel's *Messiah* the next day. Since a number of them were ushering, they slipped me in as an usher too. I loved being with these people, who were excited about what I was doing and wanted to include me in their lives. I finally felt I belonged somewhere. It felt so good! I wanted it to go on forever.

Keith and Suzanne became very close, and I learned from Suzanne that Keith didn't feel loved. She refused any elaboration (what he had disclosed to her was, I gathered, confidential), but that said it all, as far as I was concerned. I was grieved for Keith, and vowed that if I ever found the solution to this inner pain, I would let him know what it was. I knew the feeling only too well …

By the age of twenty, I had been so badly hurt that I told myself that love didn't exist. *It is just a myth that people have concocted because they are too weak to face reality*, I had thought.

But all the while, there was within me a deep sense of having been wronged. Perhaps I felt that if love didn't exist, it should have. But possibly I sensed that it did indeed exist, but that I had been firmly denied it for no reason at all, for no fault of my own. In any event,

I didn't want friends. Weren't people grossly unfair? Ultimately, they would hurt me, and I didn't want to be hurt any more. Self-sufficiency seemed to be the answer. I went on for quite some time, believing that I had discovered the truth.

By the time I turned twenty-one, however, I began to see the fallacy of this thinking. I realized that there was such a thing as meaningful relationships. Now, in Victoria, I could no longer deny it. I wanted to connect with others who valued and enjoyed me.

As time passed, however, I became more and more apprehensive. Though these friends were very positive toward me, they seemed to have such great expectations regarding my composing. What if I didn't fulfill them? What if I disappointed them, and their support turned into contempt and disgust? I couldn't bear the thought of their rejection. I felt backed up against a wall. I began to panic.

For some reason, I became particularly afraid of Stephen. But why? Perhaps because I felt so inadequate compared to him. Perhaps I felt I was already failing to live up to his expectations. After all, I no longer took piano lessons from Mr. Nickel, something he probably disapproved of. Whatever the reasons, fear him I did. I feared he no longer esteemed me as highly as he had in the beginning. And I feared he would turn the others against me.

the circle

Scars from the past played a big role. I anticipated rejection because I had learned to expect it. My experiences told me: live up to the expectations of those who esteem you or face emotional devastation. By now, I would rather die than be rejected again. For a fear greater than death tormented me: the fear that I was not loved.

On one hand, I tried to be extraordinary, composing as much as I possibly could. During restful moments away from the piano, I would visualize great success. On the other hand, I began to take pleasure at the thought of dying young. I would imagine I had died of some fatal disease and could hear them lamenting upon my death, "What a great composer she might have been had she lived!" A wave of relief would sweep over me. I hadn't had a chance to disappoint them. Now their enthusiasm could never turn to contempt.

The weeks passed. More and more, I wrote music to gain the esteem of others. Yet the acclaim of other people could never fill my soul. Surely I had gone a step backward since coming to Victoria. Should I return to Saskatoon? *Just what should I do?* I wondered.

I felt headed for a nervous breakdown, and wanted to run away and hide. Heaven forbid that they should find out how weak and frightened I was! Maybe if I went back to Saskatoon and only corresponded from a distance, I could conceal it. Surely if I stayed, it was only a matter of time before I would disappoint and disillusion these special friends.

Another consideration seemed to favor my leaving. Maybe if I lived far away from them, this nagging concern with what they thought of me would gradually disappear. I certainly hoped so; it wasn't doing me one iota of good. Though in many ways I wanted to stay–I absolutely loved Victoria–I finally decided to move back to Saskatoon.

"You're going back to Saskatoon?" asked Neal one day, after hearing the news.

"I am," I replied.

"But you need to be in a place where a lot is happening musically, a place that's stimulating. What are you going to do back in Saskatoon?"

I had no comment. He looked sullen and disappointed.

"You'll miss the big première," he pointed out, for Stephen was due to play my set of pieces in the festival in about another month. But again, I didn't have much to say.

The night before I left, I had quite a lengthy talk with Keith.

"No one cares about me," he shared with me. The agony within him was coming to the surface. He had been feeling this way before meeting Suzanne. But since Suzanne had broken off their romance and now wanted to be "just friends," he had become very depressed.

As we talked, it became apparent to me that he was contemplating suicide.

"I guess I'm pretty messed up," he confessed.

"I've had some pretty heavy emotional problems myself," I admitted. I described a little of what they had been.

"Someday we'll meet again, and we'll both have straightened these problems out," he reflected. But he didn't sound too hopeful.

And with that, I left.

CHAPTER 2

The Big Blunder

"What the wicked fears will come upon him."
—Prov. 10:24a

I gazed at the slush and dirty snow that covered the streets of Saskatoon. *What a letdown from Victoria!* I thought, for a beautiful spring had blossomed in that lovely city back in February. I thought of the people I had left behind. How I missed them!

"You're going through a grief reaction," a doctor told me, "similar to what a person goes through when there's a death in the family. Your emotional energies have been withdrawn from these people. You will be grieved until you, once again, put those energies into new, meaningful relationships."

But I didn't want to replace those relationships with other, new relationships. Those friends were irreplaceable. Yet so great was my fear of losing their esteem, that I soon felt threatened where no threat actually existed.

As the time that Stephen was to have played my two pieces in the festival passed, I wrote him a letter asking him how it had gone. But he did not reply. I interpreted this to mean that he no longer considered me worth the time of day. Enraged, I wrote him an angry letter, telling him he was the most conceited and inconsiderate person I knew and demanded my compositions back, plus a book I had lent him.

Of course, I was completely blind to how unfair and inconsiderate *I* was being. After all, what had he done to deserve this? Not a thing! Yet, to me it looked like rejection, for people who fear rejection will imagine they see rejection everywhere, though it isn't real. A sad paradox was doing its deadly work: the self-defeating nature of fear would soon destroy the very support I so desperately felt I needed and could not live without. Scripture says, "What the wicked fears will come upon him" (Prov. 10:24a). I had made it clear that I was upset. What was unclear was that a profound fear of rejection was rocking my whole foundation.

I spent the summer working part-time and doing a study of Canadian poetry. I had written a few poems in Victoria, but now I pursued poetry and short-story writing with an interest I'd never had before. I joined the Saskatoon Poet's Club. This enabled me to meet other writers and to receive some excellent constructive criticism from the editor of *Grain Magazine*, who always attended these meetings. Though I usually felt inspired any time I sat down to do any literary writing, it was a very different story when I sat down at the piano to compose.

Why, why is my creative spirit so frequently barren, like a desert wasteland? I wondered in exasperation. How could I accomplish anything in composing, when my ability to compose went up and down like a roller coaster? How could my joy in life, which depended on the excitement of composing, be sustained? *I should be able to produce, I have to be able to, or I'm worth nothing*, I thought. Yet, because I could not, I became gripped with the fear that I had no worth. I expressed this frustration in the following poem:

THE COMPOSER CANNOT

Before, excited by his own making.
With power, courage, projecting his reality,
Unafraid to belong to it.

What has happened?
Why has he become like a deformed pipe,
Twisted around itself with a deadly grip,
Yet unable to hold on—

Slipping, falling now
Down a gradual quieting
to silence.

To escape this unbearable dilemma, I withdrew into daydreams. I imagined myself dying of some terrible illness, and felt deeply comforted. In fact, so strong had this desire become, that it now dominated my life. I would have done almost *anything* to get such an illness. Strangely enough, I *was* losing my health – dramatically. Extreme fatigue now plagued my life and something was obviously wrong with my hands.

"Looks like rheumatoid arthritis, Bev," my doctor told me, worriedly. I'd been told the same thing six years earlier. Following a minor injury in gym class, I had experienced unusual symptoms in my legs. I had seen a doctor, tests had been done, and I had been told I had rheumatoid arthritis. After a few months, the symptoms had disappeared and the diagnosis had been withdrawn. Now symptoms had recurred, this time primarily in my hands. Again, the assessment was rheumatoid arthritis. Six years earlier, the diagnosis had shaken me and I had feared becoming crippled. Now the diagnosis disappointed me. I had hoped that it was something terminal.

Christmas arrived. I thought I'd phone Suzanne, who hadn't written for quite some time. We had a pleasant enough chat. (I deliberately covered up how sick

I was feeling.) But our conversation left me disturbed. She hinted that people had been gossiping about me. Then I realized that some heated words had been spoken in protest to the rash letter I had sent Stephen.

Shortly after this, I read *A Guide to Rational Living* by Albert Ellis, a well-known American psychologist. Unlike some psychologists, who contend that one must not repress anger but must learn to handle it and cope with it, Ellis very emphatically maintains that all talk of "handling" and "coping" with anger is nonsense. One must stop demanding and commanding. As I read through his book, I knew he was right.

I had been dead wrong in exploding at Stephen. Scripture says, "An angry man stirs up strife, and a furious man abounds in transgression" (Prov. 29:22 NKJ). James writes, "My dear brothers, take note of this: Everyone should be quick to listen, slow to speak and slow to become angry, for man's anger does not bring about the righteous life that God desires" (James 1:19-20 NIV). Solomon wrote, "Do not hasten in your spirit to be angry, for anger rests in the bosom of fools" (Eccles. 7:9 NKJ).

Dark clouds of guilt and condemnation now hung over my life. I felt like a ruined person. I hated myself passionately. *I deserve to die,* I thought. *I'm such an awful person.* I became dangerously suicidal because I couldn't stand myself, because I believed they all hated me, and because physically, I felt absolutely wretched.

I wrote one of the girls in Victoria, saying what a rough time I was having. Without intending to, I offended everyone. Nothing I had written so far was so misunderstood as this letter!

"Well, I was sure surprised to hear from *you!*" she wrote back, making no effort to conceal her contempt. Although she made some positive suggestions, what she said near the end amounted to this: "What a person *does* shows his very *core!*"

And that was that. My mistake in exploding at Stephen was final, as far as she was concerned. It was unforgivable. I would be given no mercy. My lack of worth as a person was settled forever.

THE ABYSS

Blurred, incomprehensible messages
from somewhere
Penetrate the walls of my consciousness,
Only to fade into nothingness.

My thoughts dart back and forth like little arrows,
Making futile pecks in the walls of some enclosed cave.

Dripping from an unknown crevice
Are the poisonous drops of a malice
Too painful to bare,
Too rank to inhale,
Too ghastly to see.

The Big Blunder

And that ever-steady, never dimming patter,
Slowly wears through the dusty floor
A narrow passage downward
That penetrates ever-deeper
as the moments pass.

A dreamy, blank sensation
Clouds over this deep, pitted pain
Like a veil pulled over a nervous, wailing infant,
Too weak, too immature to persist.

So the crying ceases.

Ah! So calm, so quiet.

Yet somewhere I see a dim light
Trying to pass through a discolored window,
And, as if behind a screen,
The rays scattered in all directions,
Confused, dismembered.

One word wells up in my mind,
Pushing out all others:
The word *no.*
Softly but firmly, no.
For no apparent reason,
Without definite meaning,
Yet I am sure of it.
No.......No.
Absolutely never.

Nor do I care.
Just don't demand that of me because I won't.
I just wanted to make that clear.
Do you understand?
What's that, you say?

I…can't hear you
But no matter.

I can't even see you now;
I guess you've gone away
Unless you were never really here—
I can't remember for sure.

Can you come back tomorrow?
No, don't bother. I won't be here myself.

Strange, it's getting so dark, so early.
I only just got here.
I don't think it's been bright all day—
But it could just be my sunglasses,
If I'm wearing them.

I think these are just my ordinary glasses—
But I don't have ordinary glasses!
So it must have been dull all day.
Always is around here.

Yet it sure seems like it.

The Big Blunder

You're not listening again.
But don't bother.
It's too fatiguing.

Even the small light out on the water is exhausted,
Doing its slow, hopeless turns,
Out of tune,
Out of phase,
Like the light on a worn-out ambulance,
Arriving too late.

CHAPTER 3

An Awakening in my soul

"He who turns a sinner from the error of his way will save his soul from death."

—James 5:20a

W hat do you daydream about?" asked my psychiatrist as I leaned back against the huge easy chair in her office.

"That I'm dying of some fatal disease," I replied.

"You mustn't like yourself very much," she concluded. Well, that was quite likely. "Daydreaming is like taking poison. It destroys a person's ability to concentrate. It can break a person's contact with reality to such a degree that a person can actually go insane," she explained.

You mean, I could lose my sanity? I thought. *Wow!* I was a serious daydreamer, daydreaming to music at least four hours a day! I explained that I was *obsessed* with this fantasy of dying of a terminal illness.

"Obsessions are more difficult to overcome than depression," she explained. I found her statement very interesting.

"Do you have any friends?"

"One."

"Only one?"

"Only one," I insisted.

"You live a very self-centered life, don't you?" she asked gently. I nodded, realizing for the first time in my life that I *was* self-centered, *very* self-centered.

"It doesn't work, does it?" she asked.

"No, I guess not," I confessed. Another realization dawned on me: *it didn't work!*

"You need to reach out more to other people," she pointed out. "Do you love anyone?" she wanted to know.

I answered that I loved my one friend. She sounded skeptical.

"I love those people in Victoria," I offered.

"You didn't love them," she objected.

It was true. The most I had been able to offer them was a very selfish kind of love. I didn't need them because I loved them; I loved them because I needed them. Because I needed them, I feared losing them. I discussed my unrighteous reaction to Stephen's simply not replying to a letter, which should have been no big deal. She offered some valuable insight.

"The conscious mind is only able to handle a certain level of fear. Then it turns to anger."

Then it dawned on me that the anger I had felt was actually fear—fear that he no longer considered me important or worth the time and effort to respond to my letter. This fear had grown so big that it had exploded into rage.

"You didn't want them to know you were afraid?"

I shook my head.

"One thing is true of everyone who comes here to see me. They all have fear."

I shared with her how suicidal I was.

"You might be jumping from the frying pan into the fire," she warned. "Hell is a real place, a place of punishment. To die rebelling against God and without Christ as one's Savior is to spend eternity in unspeakable torment." I had always viewed suicide as a guaranteed way to end all suffering. No one had ever pointed out to me that this may not be so. I was startled.

She gave me plenty to think about. From our discussions and from literature she asked me to read, I discovered that we all long to be loved. Yet, if we seek to satisfy that longing by seeking others who will love us, the paradoxical result will be, not the fulfillment of that need, but only a greater desolation, only a greater sense of estrangement and rejection. Why? We have made ourselves the center of our world, and though there is a reason why we have done so (the pain within us is demanding the focus of our attention), it will destroy us. It is designed to destroy us. If a person, on the other hand, forgets his own needs and focuses on the happiness and fulfillment of his fellow man, he will become a fulfilled human being whose potential can flower and whose character can reach maturity.

But we are able to love others this way only if we have first become aware that God loves us! This is the source of our cup that overflows with love and grace. 1 John 4:19 says, "We love because He first loved us" (NIV). This is where most people fail. This realization has never dawned on their souls. I discovered something that amazed me: he who tries to save his life will lose it, but he who loses it for His sake will save it. This paradox had escaped me. Yet I couldn't see how I could ever become such a selfless, loving person.

I began to realize that perhaps there really is a personal Creator who feels joy and heartbreak, peace and distress, who becomes angry when provoked, and who is moved with compassion toward the suffering and the sick. After all, how could we, who are very personal, have been created by something completely impersonal? Can we really possess this quality if our Creator does not possess it?

"The whole direction of your life needs to change," my psychiatrist informed me, and she was right. I didn't need to turn over a new leaf; I needed a new life.

Then she recommended I read *Mere Christianity* by C. S. Lewis. A new understanding came to me as I read through its pages. Christianity had always seemed terribly irrational to me. Now, as the divine plan opened before me, I saw it as very rational. Surely life was more than one big accident. It was more than a series of thousands of accidents, which I had been calling "fate."

Surely, *that* would have been the epitome of senselessness. But no, it had been brought into being by a master Creator for a definite purpose. People without God may have personal goals that are very helpful to mankind. One may want to find the cure for cancer; another may want to abolish poverty. Another may want to be a really fine architect, or piano teacher, or lawyer. Yet now I could see that life had a much greater purpose than this.

For the first time in my life I realized that there *is* a God. Suddenly, I *knew* there is an eternity beyond this life. The heavens seemed to open before my eyes, and I beheld the magnificence of the Lord. I gasped in awe. Me? Struck by the grandeur and beauty of the Lord? How could this possibly have happened? It happened because God had revealed Himself to me. When God chooses to reveal Himself, even the gates of hell cannot prevail against Him.

I became hungry with a desire to know this God. I began reading the Bible three hours a day. As I searched His Word, a new hope entered my life. My suicidal desires left, though my desire for a fatal disease remained.

I made several Christian friends. A friend of my sister's, who directed a church choir, phoned me one afternoon. He needed someone to play the organ for one of the Sunday services. Could I help out? Though I'd never met the fellow, I accepted immediately.

So began a new and edifying relationship. As we became more acquainted, we discovered that we had gone to the same high school, had been in the same grade, and knew a lot of the same people. He'd been involved in drugs and crime and had even been the leader of a gang. He had been seeing the same psychiatrist I was seeing, and she had brought him to faith in Christ! We went out together frequently, and this gave me the opportunity to ask him all the questions I'd been wondering about, such as "Who was this Jesus anyway?"

"Well, you see, what He did was this," he explained, as we sat sipping Coke at the A&W. "As He hung there on the cross, all the sins of every human being, from the beginning of time to the end, were upon Him."

I made a great effort to grasp what he meant. I tried to picture Jesus on the cross. On Him were all the sins of every person, past, present, and future? I'd never heard this before. I struggled to comprehend how He could even have known what they all were.

An Awakening in My Soul

But God saw to it that the plan of redemption was explained to me. These are the key points. Originally, the parents of the human race, Adam and Eve, were created perfect and were without sin. But then they disobeyed God. From that moment on, man became sinful. Every person born since has been born dead in trespasses and sin. Fallen man is an enemy of God. He is a child of the devil. Because God is absolutely holy, He cannot fellowship with that which is unholy. And because God is just, He cannot let sin go unpunished. In His eyes, sin is an extremely serious thing - so serious, that its penalty is death. Speaking through the prophet Ezekiel, God declared, "The soul who sins will die" (Ez. 18:4b). The apostle Paul writes, "For the wages of sin is death, but the free gift of God is eternal life in Christ Jesus our Lord" (Rom. 6:23). Without a redeemer, a person is headed for everlasting punishment. This means spending eternity in the lake of fire, being tormented day and night forever.

But God loves man so much, He sent His own Son to take the penalty for man's sin. As He died on the cross, He died in man's place, allowing all the wrath of God that burned against man on account of his sin to fall on Him. Speaking of the coming Messiah, the prophet Isaiah wrote, "He was wounded for our transgressions, He was bruised for our iniquity" (Isa. 53:5a NKJ). Further on in the same chapter, Isaiah continues, "My righteous Servant shall justify many, for He shall bear their iniquities" (Isa. 53:11b). The word translated "bear" in this verse, means "to bear as a substitute" and "to completely remove." When a person repents of his sins and receives Jesus as his Lord and Savior, this redemptive work that Christ accomplished at Calvary is applied to his life. In the reckoning of God, the penalty for all his sins has been paid for by Jesus, who has removed them as far as the east is from the west. He is no longer God's enemy, but instead becomes His child, who has been forgiven and redeemed. Paul writes, "Therefore, if anyone is in Christ, he is a new creation; the old has gone, the new has come!" (2 Cor. 5:17). Provided he lives a holy life, he will enjoy God's fellowship all the remaining days of his life and will spend eternity with the Lord in heaven. If he fails to walk in righteousness, however, he will be sentenced to hell with all other evil doers, for without holiness, no one shall see the Lord (Heb. 12:14).

Some insist that Jesus was a great moral teacher, but not the Son of God. Yet Jesus claimed:

1. **He had always existed:** "Jesus said to them, 'Truly, truly, I say to you, before Abraham was born, I am'" (John 8:58).
2. **He has authority to forgive sins:** To a paralyzed man, Jesus declared, "Take courage, My son, your sins are forgiven" (Matt. 9:2b). When some of the scribes present thought He was

blaspheming, Jesus said, "In order that you may know that the Son of Man [Jesus] has authority on earth to forgive sins" – then He said to the paralytic – "Rise, take up your bed, and go home" (Matt. 9:6). Quickened by the healing power of God, the man arose and went home.

3. **He and the Father are One:** "I and the Father are one." The Jews took up stones again to stone Him. Jesus answered them, "I showed you many good works from the Father; for which of them are you stoning Me?" The Jews answered Him, "For a good work we do not stone You, but for blasphemy; and because You, being a man, make Yourself out to be God" (John 10:30-33).

4. **He is the *only* way to the Father:** "I am the way, and the truth, and the life; no one comes to the Father, but through Me" (John 14:6).

5. **His death would be a ransom for many:** "The Son of Man did not come to be served, but to serve, and to give His life a ransom for many" (Matt. 20:28).

6. **God the Father has committed all judgment into His hands:** "For not even the Father judges anyone, but He has given all judgment to the Son, in order that all may honor the Son, even as they honor the Father" (John 5:22-23).

7. **All who believe in Him will have eternal life:** "For God so loved the world, that He gave His only

begotten Son, that whoever believes in Him should not perish, but have eternal life" (John 3:16).

If He isn't who He clearly claimed to be, then His claims are false. If they are false, He either knew they were false, making Him a liar, or He didn't know, making Him a madman. But a great moral teacher He couldn't be! As C.S. Lewis writes:

> I am trying here to prevent anyone saying the really foolish thing that people often say about Him: 'I'm ready to accept Jesus as a great moral teacher, but I don't accept His claim to be God.' That is the one thing we must not say. A man who was merely a man and said the sort of things Jesus said would not be a great moral teacher. He would either be a lunatic—on a level with the man who says he is a poached egg—or else he would be the Devil of Hell. You must make your choice. Either this man was, and is, the Son of God: or else a madman or something worse. You can shut Him up for a fool, you can spit at Him and kill Him as a demon; or you can fall at His feet and call Him Lord and God. But let us not come with any patronising nonsense about His being a great human teacher. He has not left that open to us. He did not intend to.[1]

I found *Screwtape Letters,* another work by C. S. Lewis, very enlightening as well. This book is a fictional story that portrays a senior demon teaching a junior demon the different techniques that can be used to turn Christians away from God. If successfully tripped, such believers are no longer a threat to the kingdom of darkness. From this highly insightful and humorous account, I became aware of the spiritual battle that people are in every day, and some of the strategies the devil has devised in order to defeat Christians.

As I went into His house regularly to play the organ for the services, I heard His word and received it eagerly. It had become alive! Standing beside this young man, our heads bowed, I heard, for the first time, someone actually *pray* the Lord's Prayer with all his heart. The songs he chose for the choir to sing were superb! I'd never heard such beautiful church music!

I soon became close friends with one of the girls in the choir. I learned so much from her! She had been an alcoholic until the Lord changed her life. She explained to me that she tried to turn every situation into a *giving* situation. I thought very deeply about this remark.

Another Christian friend I made at this time explained to me that becoming a Christian meant entering into a relationship with our Creator. *What a novel concept!* I thought. *Is such a thing actually possible?*

"Say out loud to yourself, several times throughout the day, 'God loves me,'" suggested my psychiatrist. She also urged me to completely surrender to the Lord and to strive to live a holy, consecrated life.

During this period, I had another experience that made quite an impression on me. While going about the duties of my job, I suddenly became aware of God's presence, and that nothing was hidden from Him. He knew my every thought, every moment of the day. As the psalmist wrote:

> O Lord, You have searched me and You know me.
> You know when I sit and when I rise;
> You perceive my thoughts from afar.
> You discern my going out and my lying down;
> You are familiar with all my ways.
> Before a word is on my tongue
> You know it completely, O Lord.
>
> —Ps. 139:1–4 NIV

But as I probed and searched, doubts assailed my mind. I couldn't decide which was right: my long-standing atheistic view of life or what the Bible proclaimed as truth. Most of all, I couldn't understand this Jesus business. *Why does one have to be a Christian? I wondered. What is wrong with other religions such as Islam and Buddhism? Is the Bible really the word of God, or is it man-made?* I couldn't decide. And I found the idea that man is a sinner, that his heart is deceitful and desperately wicked, very, very difficult to accept. This would have implied that he needed to be forgiven and restored. I didn't want to admit that I needed such things. "For the message of the cross is foolishness to those who are perishing" (1 Cor. 1:18a NIV). And I was perishing.

Then, too, I wanted first and foremost to become a productive composer. The things of God were secondary. Because I only sought God as a means to an end, He was unable to give me the inner peace and stability that would have given me the freedom in the area of composing I so longed for.

Finally, I wanted to retain my "right" to hate someone if I wanted to. Believers are commanded to walk in love. *Is that what I want to do?* I wondered.

With this unwillingness, and with my questions going unanswered, I decided, *I will leave my decision for or against Christ until the very end of my life, when I will have to decide. In the meantime, I will go my own way.*

CHAPTER 4

ɪs ᴛʜɪs ᴛʜᴇ ᴇɴᴅ?

"Be careful how you think; your life is shaped by your thoughts."

—Prov. 4:23 Good News Version

I watched my rheumatologist as she gave me a routine checkup. *Why does she look so grave and serious?* I wondered. She left the room for a moment and then came back with several other doctors. They also checked me over and asked some questions. The rheumatology nurse, who had followed them into the room, looked at me with great pity. Something was very wrong. My whole being was on the alert.

"I think we've been on the wrong track," said my specialist nervously. "I don't think it's rheumatoid arthritis. It looks like another illness."

45

Though she did her best to control herself, I could tell she was shaken.

"What's this illness called?" I asked the nurse, as she escorted me down the hospital corridor to the test lab.

She paused and then answered, "Systemic lupus."

The word *lupus* stabbed me like a knife. This serious illness, eventually confirmed by tests, is considered terminal.

I reeled with shock. I felt as though the door had been slammed in my face. "If you're going to wait until the end of your life to come to Me, I'll end it now," God seemed to be saying. I went home and listened to the song, "Come Unto Him," from Handel's *Messiah*, again and again. The words to this beautiful choral number are:

> Come unto Him all ye that labor,
> Come unto Him, ye that are heavy laden,
> And He will give you rest.
> Take His yoke upon you and learn of Him,
> For He is meek and lowly of heart,
> And ye shall find rest,
> And ye shall find rest unto your souls.

Based on Matt. 11:28-29 (KJV), this choral number encourages those who are heavy laden to come to Jesus, and He will give them rest. That night, and the next, and the next, I cried out to God to give me peace, but peace did not come. "Why don't you answer me?" I hollered out to God, but it seemed as though heaven's door had been shut. Again I merely sought the comforts of God (i.e. His peace) rather than the God of all comfort.

I felt more and more devastated as the days passed. A week passed, then two, then three. After four weeks, the shock eased. Though at times I continued to feel shattered, at other times I felt a deep satisfaction. A silent smile, a secret joy was emerging within me. I now had the fatal disease I had wanted so badly. *This is too good to be true!* I thought.

A great desire to return to Victoria rose up within me. I just *had* to see those people again! The fact that they had no desire to see me just didn't register. I was in complete denial. So I arranged to make the trip. I didn't realize that I was fulfilling a vow I had made when I left Victoria, the vow that I would return when I was either famous or terminally ill. Now I was returning, and I was terminally ill.

In Victoria, after a cold initial reception, they warmed up to me. The first people I saw were Keith and Charles, so the three of us went out for coffee. Shortly afterward, I visited Suzanne, who was now in her third year at the university. During the previous year, trying to study and practice as many hours as possible, she had been getting only three or four hours of sleep each night. When summer came and she returned home to Calgary, she slept fifteen hours a day or more. She just couldn't make out on any less. Her dad had sent her to the doctor, who ran many tests but concluded that she was simply exhausted from chronic lack of sleep. Her dad had given her an ultimatum: she was to get the rest she needed each night during the school year or he would not send her back to the university.

When the subject of the nasty letter I'd written Stephen came up, she commented, "Such an attack gives the other person the right to attack you in return." This confirmed my suspicion that he had retaliated with a few scalding words of his own. Naturally, the others sympathized with *him*. I replied that hopefully he had recognized that what I had said about him wasn't true and had been able to shrug it off.

One afternoon, when I was busy on the piano in one of the practice rooms at the Conservatory, who opened the door and stood there with a big smile but Stephen! My eyes shifted back and forth nervously, unsure of what to expect. Then he came and sat down on the piano bench beside me and embraced me! I couldn't believe it! After this beautiful embrace, he invited me downstairs for a cup of tea! I followed him down, and everything was wonderful for about five minutes when I blundered *again!* He graciously offered to return the book he had borrowed from me, but I replied, rather curtly, "Keep it." Right away, he was offended (who would blame him?) and what could have been a beautiful reconciliation was spoiled. What a lost opportunity! It was heart-breaking and incomprehensible.

Lori and I drew closer together. Once I returned home, we kept in touch through letters. On the last day of my visit, I shared with Stephen the seriousness of my illness. He took it very hard, making the remark, "Life doesn't make any sense at all. It makes you wonder how you got here in the first place."

Meanwhile, I became frightened at the prospect of dying. Though at times I still derived pleasure from my plight, at other times I panicked, and wondered desperately if there was *any* way my life could be saved. One night I cried out to God, "Don't let me die!"

It so happened that a young man from Japan lived in the apartment right across the hall from me. One day we were discussing health problems. He shared with me that he had had very severe asthma at one time while still living in Japan. There, people often battled illness by going on a fast, followed by a relatively strict diet so that the benefits gained during the fast would not be lost.

He had fasted ten days on water and then had driven to a fasting clinic in order to come off the fast. This ensured that he didn't overeat and that he ate only the right foods. He never had asthma again! He also stressed that people with many different types of illnesses used these methods with great results. Eager to help me in any way that he could, he went to a health food store and bought me the book, *Fasting Can Save Your Life* by Herbert Shelton, one of the great pioneers of fasting in the United States. He operated a fasting clinic just south of San Antonio, Texas, which he called a health school. Here, a person could fast for an extended period of time under proper medical supervision. As he had been operating this fasting clinic for many years, he had witnessed many people improve or fully recover from a wide variety of health problems. He wrote of many of these cases in *Fasting Can Save Your Life.*

As I read this book, I realized that recovery was within reach, contrary to medical opinion. New hope flooded my being as I read of people with a wide variety of medical problems overcoming those problems by fasting, followed by a strict diet of raw vegetables, fruit, and nuts. I thought I had nothing to lose. I phoned Shelton's health school to enquire about coming to the clinic to do a fast. As there were no present openings, I was put on a waiting list. In the meantime, I thought I'd try drinking only tomato juice and water. The results were almost unbelievable: by the fourth day, the overpowering fatigue that had been plaguing my life left! My life had suddenly returned to normal!

But then this Japanese fellow persuaded me to break the fast, insisting that it should be done on water only. So I broke the fast in the worst possible way—with a pizza—and by the next day, the fatigue had returned. From what I know now, I am convinced that had I continued the fast for another six days, then come off it properly–with small quantities of fruit the first day, then continuing with a diet consisting primarily of raw vegetables, fruit, and nuts–I could have achieved a permanent remission in a very short period of time. (This procedure brought resounding results when the illness became active a second time, throughout 1984-86. This time I drank lemon juice. Remarkably, by the fifth day, the illness went into remission, a remission which has lasted to this day.)

Soon the Shelton Clinic phoned, saying that an opening had become available. I could come immediately. I quickly informed my piano students and flew to San Antonio, where a life-changing experience awaited me.

When I arrived, I began at once a fast on water only. Each afternoon, I attended a lecture dealing with various aspects of rebuilding health. I learned that the best way to regain health is to start by going on a fast so that the body could eliminate the toxins that had built up. In the absence of food, the body begins to feed on its own tissues to survive. The first tissues to be "eaten" are diseased parts, such as inflammation and tumors. (Of course, anyone taking cortisone should never discontinue his medication suddenly in order to go on a fast. The results can be fatal.)

Lectures also explained how long a person should fast, how the fast should be broken, why protein from raw nuts is superior to protein from animal sources, and why raw food is superior to cooked food. The speaker emphasized the importance of removing harmful foods and replacing them with natural, whole foods. After all, what makes people sick in the first place? Is it not, in many cases, excessive amounts of white bread, desserts, ice cream, soft drinks, salty foods, fried foods, and processed and refined foods? Too much protein—especially animal protein—is also very harmful.

The claim: many diseases considered incurable can be overcome with fasting and diet. When I began my fast, my parents back in Saskatoon, decided to fast the first three days along with me, in sympathy. My dad had been a heavy smoker for years, and his repeated efforts to quit had all failed. Yet, after fasting on water for only three days, all desire for cigarettes disappeared, and he never smoked again as long as he lived! He wasn't even trying to quit! I explained to him over the phone that some people come to the clinic to quit smoking, as it is a known fact that people can become free of this addiction by going on a fast. This amazed him.

As I fasted day after day, I didn't really feel any better, however. Unlike the tomato juice fast, my fatigue didn't disappear. Thoroughly exhausted, I slept fifteen hours a day. As I lay in bed, I wondered what the outcome of this fasting and diet regime would be. Would it work? Would I recover fully? It was hard to imagine. Plus, from the lectures, it sounded as though the diet would have to be so strict that I'd never be able to follow it.

Sometimes I dreamed that I had eaten some chocolate cake and had completely ruined the fast. When I awoke, I'd be so relieved. I was still on track after all! I came to know Betty, a woman from Chicago who suffered from arthritis of the spine. We had both started our fasts at the same time. She had been superb at baking. She often described one of her favorite dishes. Then she would catch herself and ask, "Are we talking about food again?"

But at times, recovery seemed meaningless. *Why do I want to recover?* I wondered. *What is the point?* I knew beyond a doubt that something was seriously lacking in my life and to continue without it was futile. Yet the prospect of hell on the other side of death haunted me. What if hell is a real place? I shuddered. *If anyone's destined to hell, it's me,* I thought. I felt neither alive nor dead but as though I were hovering about in some existence that lay between the two, some thin thread along which one could pass from one to the other. An eternity in hell? I trembled. I could sense death waiting for me at the doorstep. But I could hear the quiet, still voice of God saying, "Please, please accept My Son!"

I won't blackmail God, I thought. *I'm not going to come to Jesus just because I want some last minute deal with God that will keep me from going to hell.*

"Please accept My Son!" He continued to plead. I could sense His broken voice and tear-filled eyes. "Whoever denies the Son does not have the Father; the one who confesses the Son has the Father also" (1 John 2:23). Isaiah the prophet had written, "Seek the Lord while He may be found; Call upon Him while He is near" (Isa. 55:6).

"I can't. I'm not ready," I answered.

But the words of my doctor also troubled me so that I could not rest. "You can follow the diet 100%," she had said, "but unless you solve your emotional problems, you will not recover."

I had sensed this intuitively. But to hear it from a doctor made it worse. My growing awareness that psychological factors could play a major role in lupus disturbed me. It was true that the onset of the illness had actually occurred in high school. After being dormant for six years, it became active shortly after I moved back to Saskatoon from Victoria. Then it had turned into a major illness that September, only nine months after I first began to imagine and desire a fatal disease! Though psychological factors hadn't been solely responsible for this illness, I couldn't help wonder, *Was there a connection between this wish and this illness becoming active? If so, what a wreck I'd made of my life!*

But is God the answer? I wondered. I tried to tell myself there is no such thing as a personal God, that people had taken the Bible too literally. Some impersonal "force" is behind everything—that's all. After all, I didn't *want* to think there really is a God to whom I am accountable. But I knew this wasn't true. I *knew* there is a God. He had shown Himself to me, and no argument, no line of reasoning could take me back to my comfortable atheism, though I longed to return to it. Whether I liked it or not, He had shattered that land forever, and there was no return.

The fool says in his heart, "There is no God."

—Ps. 14:1a NIV

CHAPTER 5

My Turning Point

"I am the way, the truth, and the life. No one comes to the Father except through Me."

—John 14:6 NKJV

Several months passed. I was back in Saskatoon. I felt awful, for the 21-day water fast had left me very depleted. Nonetheless, I saw some notable results from the fast:

1. The severe Sjögren's Syndrome that I'd been diagnosed with in August 1976–causing dry eyes and a dry mouth–completely disappeared, never to return. Dr. Shelton had written in his book that the eye diseases that disappeared during a fast had to be seen to be believed!

2. The abdominal pain I'd experienced after every meal also disappeared, with little trouble thereafter. Betty, who had also experienced extreme pain after eating, said the same thing after her fast: the pain was gone!

3. The extreme body odor caused by the disease had completely vanished.

4. The muscle spasms I had experienced in my legs disappeared.

5. Certain blood tests that had been abnormal prior to the fast were now normal.

One day, at the local health food store, I noticed a little book entitled, *The Grape Cure*. It had been written by a woman who had recovered from cancer by eating nothing but grapes, followed by a diet of predominantly raw vegetables. (Eating the same vegetables cooked had failed to restore her to health.) I bought it and found it fascinating. In one of the books by Shelton that I had purchased at his health school, he discussed different mono-diets, including the grape diet. He claimed that it had produced excellent results in people with cancer as well as those with rheumatism, liver problems, and even alcoholics. "These fruits are rich in organic salts, which are liberated during digestion, and supply the body with the elements necessary to the neutralization and chemicalization of the toxins preparatory to their elimination," Shelton explains in his book, *The Hygienic System, Vol. 2: Orthotrophy.*[2]

I considered it carefully. Then I decided to try it. Within a week the fatigue left, and I enjoyed weeks and weeks of feeling great. Though it would be another eight to nine months before I would feel great on a consistent basis, I had definitely turned a corner. I knew that my cry to God, "Don't let me die," had been answered. God had slain the giant for me! It was almost too good to be true. God, Himself, had placed that young man from Japan so close by. He had used him to steer me in the right direction and ultimately, to save my life. *How He must care about me,* I thought.

Filled with gratitude toward God and with Easter approaching, I thought I would start going to church again. Perhaps I would understand the resurrection. I decided to attend Faith Baptist Church, where a friend of mine from high school went to church. The pastor, Rev. Henry Blackaby, is now well-known for his best-selling book, *Experiencing God.* Everyone just called him "Henry." I met with him during the week, and he talked to me about the Lord. My need to be made right with God became clear to me. That every person alive had sinned and needs to be redeemed is clearly taught in Scripture. "As it is written, 'There is none righteous, not even one'" (Rom. 3:10). "For all have sinned and fall short of the glory of God" (Rom. 3:23). I could do nothing to make myself right with God. I could never earn salvation through my own efforts. If I were to gain salvation and eternal life, God would have to give it to me as a gift. "For by grace you have been saved through faith; and that not of yourselves, it is the gift of God; not as a result of works, that no one should boast" (Eph. 2:8-9).

The following Sunday, I went to church. My decision for or against Christ became a life and death struggle. But God promises that "You will seek Me and find Me, when you search for Me with all your heart" (Jer. 29:13 NKJV).

Buddha died saying he had not found the way. Jesus said, "I am the way, the truth, and the life. No one comes to the Father except through Me" (John 14:6 NKJV). Scripture declares, "Salvation is found in no one else, for there is no other name under heaven given to men by which we must be saved" (Acts 4:12 NIV). When Rev. Blackaby gave the altar call, all my resistance melted, and I went forward to receive Jesus as my Lord and Savior. He did not turn me away, for He promised, "All that the Father gives Me shall come to Me, and the one who comes to Me I will certainly not cast out" (John 6:37).

A great exchange occurred. All my sin, shame, and failure were transferred to Jesus, while His righteousness, victory, and eternal life were transferred to me. A glorious thing happened. Until this moment, Satan had been my father. Now, through faith in Jesus, God became my Father! "For you are all sons of God through faith in Christ Jesus" (Gal. 3:26). My unbelief was over. His goodness had brought me to repentance. I was now reconciled to my Maker by the blood of the Lamb. Ephesians 2:13 had come to pass: "But now in Christ Jesus, you who formerly were far off have been brought near by the blood of Christ." I now had peace with God, for Scripture declares, "Therefore, having been justified by faith, we have peace with God through our Lord Jesus Christ" (Rom. 5:1). Rom. 10:9-10 promises, "If you confess with your mouth Jesus as Lord, and believe in your heart that God raised Him from the dead, you shall be saved; for with the heart man believes, resulting in righteousness, and with the mouth he confesses, resulting in salvation." I now possessed eternal life, as Jesus declared, "For God so loved the world, that He gave His only begotten Son, that whoever believes in Him should not perish, but have eternal life" (John 3:16). I was now as clay in the Potter's hands. Though much of my soul still lay in darkness, this Master Potter would lead me out of that darkness, for "God is light, and in Him is no darkness at all" (1 John 1:5b).

"For God so loved the world,
that He gave His only
begotten Son,
that whoever believes in Him
should not perish,
but have eternal life."
—John 3:16

new revelation, new instructions

"You shall be My witnesses both in Jerusalem, and in all Judea and Samaria, and even to the remotest part of the earth."

—Acts 1:8b

Not long after I had received Christ as my Lord and Savior, the Lord revealed to me that He was at work in my whole situation far more than I realized. In some way I did not yet understand, He planned to use the very problems I'd been wrestling with to bring great glory to His name. In doing so, many, many people were going to be blessed. In the spirit I could hear shouts of victory. He could reveal no more, as I would be too overwhelmed.

It all seemed too marvellous to grasp. Instead of things having happened solely because of my own folly and instability, I could now see God had a wonderful purpose for everything that had taken place. I wondered how He planned to use my situation to bring great blessing to many. But I sensed that, whatever He was planning, it would be absolutely glorious!

About a month later, I decided to make another trip to Victoria. I had arranged to stay with Lori. As it turned out, her place was really too small for two people, especially since she was preparing for an important piano exam in the near future and needed privacy to practice. Several days went by, during which I sensed that my presence was a strain.

Sunday arrived. I went to church. Afterward, I proceeded to a park to read the Bible and pray. I sought the Lord's direction as to what I should do about this situation. His answer surprised me: He showed me that I should move out and go stay at the YWCA. I replied, "Okay, I'll move out tomorrow."

But He didn't accept that. "It has to be today," He replied.

"Okay. I'll go down to the Conservatory first, then I'll go get my belongings from Lori's apartment."

"Go to her *now*," He insisted. I sensed urgency in His answer, so I agreed to go. But I was apprehensive.

"How should I tell her?" I asked the Lord. "Won't I hurt her feelings?"

"Do it with love," He answered. I did all that He asked. Several days later, I went to visit her.

"How are you?" I asked.

"Much better," she replied.

She looked it too. Then she told me what had happened.

"You know, I was sitting at the piano trying to practice. I was so tired from not being able to sleep, and my nerves were so frayed. I felt I was being tested, and I just couldn't take any more."

Her response amazed me. I hadn't realized it was *that* bad.

"I wasn't in the habit of praying, but I cried out to the Lord to help me. Then when you came in and said you'd take your things and stay at the YWCA, I felt I'd been spared."

Then I related how I'd been in the park, reading the Bible and praying, when God *told me to move out!* I related the whole conversation. She replied that she couldn't have withstood one more day! I was floored.

"You see, I didn't know that, but He did," I said in amazement.

So God had revealed Himself to Lori. I discovered that Lori was hungry to know more about God and about Jesus, so we spent considerable time talking about the Lord. "He comes not to judge the world, but to save it," I pointed out. "He doesn't love us because we are good; we become good because He loves us. He loves us into it." I explained that the Christian faith was about having a relationship with God. All this was of great interest to her, so I shared with her other things about my newfound faith.

I had a chance to share with Neal too.

"I'm thinking of writing a book," he told me.

"Oh really? What about?" I asked.

"Divorce," he replied. "I think it should be more tolerated." So we began discussing human relationships. As our discussion proceeded, I learned that he was involved in transactional analysis (TA). I had just "happened" to have read the book, *Who Says I'm Okay?* by Alan Reuter. This book is a Christian challenge to the book, *I'm Okay, You're Okay*, an enormously popular book in the 1970's, which promotes the philosophy of TA. Without rejecting everything TA says, Reuter points out that TA and Christianity perceive reality differently. TA says that you're okay, just as you are. Christianity says man has an evil nature but that God loves him and can redeem him, filling him with His worthiness. I explained to Neal that man is in need of God.

"But that means that there's a big guy and a little guy," he protested.

"Right," I answered.

"Yuck!" he balked. But even so, I sensed God was working.

Keith, whose sister had just become a Christian, was somewhat open.

"Keep talking to me," he insisted, as I paused from what I was saying about the Lord. After a bit, he confessed, "I guess I just never thought about it. There must be something to it. So many people who have had near-death experiences all say the same thing." He referred to the fact that such people describe experiences that are strangely similar, either wonderful experiences or horrific ones. (For an account of such experiences, see Dr. Maurice Rawlings book, *Beyond Death's Door.*[3])

God seemed to be working in circumstances around him too. Mrs. Nickel had just been badly hurt after driving her car into a tree. "The doctors said her accident had been the result of nervous exhaustion. That really makes you think," he reflected. I nodded, interested in his remark. I wondered what else was going through his mind.

Yes, I did have glimmer of hope, but I was too preoccupied with myself and with my health. As a result, it dominated too many conversations. Plus, because I wasn't convinced that my life was worth saving, I sought reassurance constantly, saying between the lines, "Show me that you're sad. Show me that my life is worth something to you." In plain English, I craved attention. Naturally it turned them off. Because I no longer felt as well physically, I lacked the confidence I had had previously that my recovery was assured. To make matters worse, after a week or so in Victoria, I decided to extend my stay. This I believe was a mistake.

Things had been going fairly well. But the night before I left, Keith turned on me. He was fed up with all this attention-seeking. Nor was he alone. I felt my hair stand on end as the rejection I'd been dreading hit me with great force. I was speechless. Before long, however, he softened his attitude. We talked about different things. When we parted, he offered to see me off the next day, as had Lori.

Once I was back in Saskatoon, the Lord gave me some startling instructions: choose one of them and disclose how frightened I had been of losing their esteem, to the point that I had become obsessed with wanting to die. But rather than magnify the problem, magnify the answer: declare *His love* as the power that could deliver me. "Declare it, and I'll do it," He seemed to be saying.

What a test of faith! I begged for mercy. "Don't make me tell them," I pleaded to the Lord. I didn't ever want them to find out that I wanted their support so badly, I'd rather die than lose it. Why, it was unthinkable! I was horrified. *This will be the last straw,* I thought. *They'll never speak to me again, they'll be so disgusted.*

In addition to this, I wasn't sure I wanted to lay down my self-destructive plan in favor of His plan. It wasn't easy to say no to it, after I'd been counting on it to "deliver" me for so long.

I wondered whom to tell and decided on Keith. For one thing, this was my big chance to tell him the solution to feeling unloved. For another, I reasoned that since he didn't feel loved either, he would be the least likely to hold it against me, though even to him, I was very reluctant to disclose these private things.

"Lord, I just can't do it!"

In answer to these words, a supernatural power enveloped me, like a hedge of divine protection. I could physically feel it. God seemed to be saying, "Don't be afraid. No one is going to hurt you. I'm not going to let anyone hurt you."

Though this deliverance had not yet taken place, though I felt that my admission of the wretched bondage I was in would probably be met with scorn and judgment, I obeyed the Lord.

So, I began to write. I described how, after spending most of my life on the outside, as a loner, the support and affirmation I had received at the Conservatory had given me a tremendous lift. Not only was I encouraged musically, but I finally felt I belonged somewhere. I had wanted it to go on forever. But I had become more and more fearful as time went on. Sensing the tremendous expectations that they seemed to have of me, I became terrified of disappointing them and of losing their esteem. As a result, I began to crave a fatal disease, so that I would die before I had the chance to disappoint them. I made it clear that this obsession with wanting to die had by no means been broken.

"What force, what power can save such a seemingly ruined life?" I asked. Then I answered my own question with, "the love of God. I tell you this, not so that you will feel bad (for that would be terrible), but so that you will believe." As I wrote these words, I was counting on the Lord to bring them to pass. At the end of the letter, I wanted to hastily add, "Don't tell anyone!" But the Lord stopped me.

"Don't put chains on Me. Let Me do with it as I wish," He told me. A sickening feeling swept over me as I realized that Keith would be free to tell anyone he liked, anything that was in this letter. But I sensed that it was imperative that God have His way. Eternal destinies were at stake.

"Not my will but Your will be done," I consented. And I shuddered.

CHAPTER 7

The Intervening period

*"I wait for the Lord, my soul waits, and in His word
I do hope."*

—Ps. 130:5 NKJ

Lori and I now wrote regularly. I continued to share
with her my newfound faith and sought to instruct
and encourage her to the best of my abilities. I wrestled
with her problems as though they were my own. It
helped me forget myself and think of someone else. Her
hunger for the things of God greatly encouraged me as
well. A year later, while staying at the L'Abri Fellowship
in England, she wrote me, informing me that she had
just given her life to Jesus.

For some time, it had been upon my heart to deal
with the unhappiness between Stephen and me. Though

he had been gracious almost beyond belief, even offering to play my pieces on television, I had only wounded him further in response. Praying for guidance, I wrote him a reconciliatory letter to the best of my understanding at the time. I assured him that I *did* appreciate his offer to play my pieces on TV because that's what he thought I wanted. But all I wanted was for the wounds that I had caused him to heal. Nothing more. Nothing else mattered.

Yet there was one thing I said that was completely out of line. This provocative statement ruined the entire apology and made it worthless. When I realized this several months later, I felt totally frustrated. *How could I have let the enemy trick me like this?* I wondered in exasperation. It just seemed as though I couldn't do anything right when it came to Stephen. This relationship and a number of others now lay in ruins. All these mistakes made me wonder, *How can God love **me**? Is my life even worth saving or should I be executed by a firing squad?*

During this season in my life, my local church, Faith Baptist Church, became very special to me. Lots of young people who loved the Lord came to this assembly so I made many godly friends. Again and again, I visited Pastor Blackaby in his home where he counseled me. In this supportive environment, I felt valued and loved and grew stronger in the Lord. In the meantime, Keith sent me an encouraging postcard, saying, "You're really terrific!"

Nonetheless, a conflict raged within me. Part of me was normal and wanted desperately to recover, just like anyone else would have. But another part still wanted to die. Since kidney failure or neurological complications are the most common causes of death in lupus, this side craved one of these. For a perverse love of death had become a stronghold that held me in its power. Each side wrestled against the other, struggling to prevail.

At times, I felt really guilty. I felt I had let the Lord down and that my witness to Keith and all who heard of it, would end up being a tremendous anti-witness. If I were to remain undelivered and even die as a result, it would seem to prove they were right in rejecting Christianity. After all, if my faith were powerless to rescue *me*, why should *they* want it? This troubled me greatly. At these times, all peace left me and I felt sure I was headed for damnation.

One of my friends at church suggested I take a more positive attitude toward myself.

"I'll like myself if and when I change," I replied.

"But if you liked yourself, that *would* be a change," she objected. I thought she had it backwards.

I sensed God calling me to a total commitment to Him. I became excited as I anticipated a life that would revolve around Him and nothing else, a life in which everything that I did would be to the glory of God. What a glorious existence! Yet I drew back from it. I just wasn't ready to give Him that much. Too many things of the world still appealed to me. For one thing, I still wanted the support of the Victoria circle. For another, I still wanted to compose as an end in itself, for the excitement of the creative experience. Nor were my priorities right.

Gradually, my faith grew stronger as I heard His word preached week after week and experienced answers to prayer. On a trip to Edmonton, I had lost my purse.

"Lord, arrange for Bev to get her purse back," prayed a friend of mine at prayer meeting. Her faith surprised and impressed me. Two days later, the Edmonton police phoned. They had found my purse.

Shortly after this, I had the task of looking after a ninety-four-year-old woman for several weeks. My tasks included watering her plants, inside the house and out. Under a big tree in the yard, she had a large number of potted plants. One day, on one of his frequent visits, her son spotted one that was hidden from view, one that I hadn't seen. It looked finished.

He watered it and put it on the porch where his mother wasn't able to see it. (She would have been very upset.) He hoped for the best. I prayed to the Lord. Several days went by, and the plant revived.

"Do you know what we were with that plant?" he whispered to me the next time he came over.

"What?" I asked.

"Really lucky!" he joked. But I knew it wasn't luck. The Lord was showing me that He loved me so much that I could ask anything in His name, and He would do it. For Jesus promised His disciples, "I tell you the truth, My Father will give you whatever you ask in My name" (John 16:23b NIV).

Reading the testimonies of Harold Hill and Joni Earickson (now Earickson-Tada) greatly encouraged me. I thought, *If God is great enough to bring victory to their lives, He's great enough to deliver me.* And with my illness now in remission, I felt really good.

A husband and wife ministry team came to Saskatoon that summer to minister at the Centennial Auditorium. At one of the services, they asked those who had illnesses to stand. Then the husband received a word of knowledge that one of those who had risen to their feet had both lupus and a death wish. He took authority over the death wish with strong words. I could hardly believe my ears. *You mean that God had shown him my specific struggle?* I wondered.

Because this bondage remained unbroken, I became vexed in spirit. A whole year had gone by since the Lord had promised to deliver me with His love. Why was I still bound? Why had this deliverance not taken place? Tears welled up in my eyes as I left a prayer meeting one Wednesday night. My pastor stopped to talk with me.

"There's still no victory, Henry," I said, fighting back the tears.

His gentle spirit was moved with compassion. "It's not us who are hanging on to God," he assured me. "It is God who is hanging on to us."

I was deeply comforted and treasured his words.

CHAPTER 8

free at Last

"The Son of God appeared for this purpose, that He might destroy the works of the devil."

—1 John 3:8b

That fall, I left Saskatoon for Toronto. After I'd been in Toronto about four months, I learned from a Christian friend of dynamic meetings being held every Monday night in a church close to Shephard Avenue and Yonge Street. I began attending. During the hour of beautiful anointed worship which preceded the message, I could sense the presence of God in a powerful way. As the evangelist taught on the end times, I became impressed with the close return of Christ. I thought, *Here I am, preoccupied with wanting to die of lupus, when the signs of the times are warning the whole world that He is right at the door! How can I fulfill the important work God has for me in this end-time hour if I am consumed with wanting to die?*

Gradually I realized that God would not allow me to die, that my life was of great value to Him, and that I had a very special, specific assignment to fulfill.

"Lord, make me hate this death wish," I prayed. "Make me *willing* to live, right to the very moment of Your return."

Speaking to me through His word, He told me that even the hairs on my head had been counted. For Jesus assured His disciples, "Are not two sparrows sold for a penny? Yet not one of them will fall to the ground apart from the will of your Father. And even the very hairs of your head are all numbered. So don't be afraid; you are worth more than many sparrows" (Matt. 10:29-31 NIV). *He must really care about me!* I thought. He also told me, if I sinned, to come boldly to the throne of grace and He would be faithful to forgive me completely. "For we do not have a High Priest who cannot sympathize with our weaknesses, but was in all points tempted as we are, yet without sin. Let us therefore come boldly to the throne of grace, that we may obtain mercy and find grace to help in time of need" (Heb. 4:15-16 NKJ). The word *boldly* really struck me. I wasn't to come hanging my head in shame. I wasn't to beg and plead for forgiveness, fearful that I might not obtain it. *How wonderful is His mercy!* I thought.

My will to live grew much stronger. Thoughts of death departed, and I enjoyed a period of much greater fulfillment. Immobilizing fears no longer held me bound. I reached out to people all the more, and was more blessed than ever …

Christmas drew near. But instead of making plans to go home to Saskatoon to be with family and friends for the holiday season, the Lord laid it upon my heart to stay in Toronto, where there was someone who had no one, someone who would need *me* that day. Not knowing who this was, I agreed to stay, trusting that the Lord would show me in His own good time.

Sure enough, the Lord brought an elderly woman into my life and showed me that she was the one. So I asked her if we could have Christmas dinner together. She loved the idea. We had a lovely meal and a great time at one of the hotels downtown. As we parted, she said to me, "I'm so glad we've had Christmas dinner together. Otherwise, today would have been worse than the dullest Sunday!" For her, Sunday was the loneliest day of the week. Had we not gone out for dinner together, this Christmas day would have been lonelier than the loneliest Sunday. She was so grateful and happy.

I watched her get into her taxi. Light snow fell on the quiet street. It was already dark. As her taxi drove away, tears filled my eyes. I felt like the most blessed person in the whole world. I wondered how I could ever have wanted to die.

Yet Scripture warns, "Let him who thinks he stands take heed lest he fall" (1 Cor. 10:12). One day, only two months later, I had lunch with one of the girls from the Victoria circle, who was now studying piano in Toronto.

"How's your composing?" she asked eagerly.

That was all it took. An urgent desire to die of my illness overpowered me again. I struggled against it. *I hate it! I hate it! I don't want this,* I thought, but it was all in vain. I groaned, as I saw myself being pulled back into bondage.

"Help me, Lord!" I pleaded.

After several months, I received His answer. He revealed to me, like never before, how tremendous was His love for me that He had been willing to suffer hours of excruciating pain and humiliation that I might be forgiven. What a terrible price He'd been willing to pay in order to blot out my transgressions! So great was His love, He'd been willing to be crushed for my iniquities (Isaiah 53:5b) and lay down His life, in order that I could pass from death to life. As 1 John 3:16a says, "Hereby perceive we the love of God, because He laid down His life for us" (KJV). This revelation was so profound, words cannot describe it.

Suddenly I saw the truth of His great love for me and my death wish side-by-side. My death wish shocked and appalled me. How could I wish such a vicious, contemptuous thing upon myself? I wondered. I realized with anger, that I had been deceived: deceived by demonic forces. They had known all along how precious I was to the Lord but had blinded me from the fact. Through their lies, they were trying to destroy me, for their leader, the devil, "is a liar and the father of lies" (John 8:44b).

They had been plotting to destroy me from the beginning of my life. They had robbed me of love and encouragement at home. Through several other traumatic rejection experiences, they had robbed me even more, until I no longer believed that love even existed.

Though what I needed was the Father's love, the devil had offered me a counterfeit: the high esteem of this musical circle of friends. Like every counterfeit the devil offers people, it had only served to pull me into even greater bondage and had left me feeling more unloved than ever. The devil had tricked me into acting in ways that turned these special people against me. Satan had been the author of every put-down, every false accusation, every hate-filled word spoken against me as he moved in upon me in what he hoped would drive me over the edge to suicide. It was organized crime at its highest level, and it had almost succeeded.

Jesus promised His disciples, "If you abide in My word, then you are truly disciples of Mine; and you shall know the truth, and the truth shall make you free" (John 8:31b-32). Neil Anderson, in his book, *The Bondage Breaker*, stresses the fact that since it is truth that makes us free, this implies that it is deception that holds us in bondage. As long as I believed the lie that I needed the affirmation of the Victoria circle to feel good about myself, the lie that I couldn't bear their rejection but that it was inevitable, I was paralyzed with fear and unable to get free.

But the truth of how precious I am to God now shone into my understanding like a bright light, exposing those lies and revealing their true source. As a result, the chains of bondage fell off, never to return. Knowing the truth, I became free. "If therefore the Son shall make you free, you shall be free indeed" (John 8:36). Jesus declared, "The thief comes only to steal, and kill, and destroy; I came that they might have life, and might have it abundantly" (John 10:10).

Jesus tells us what truth is. Before He went to the cross, He prayed to the Father concerning His disciples, "Sanctify them in the truth; Thy word is truth" (John 17:17). God's word is truth and it is alive and full of power, "for the word of God is living and powerful, and sharper than any two-edged sword" (Heb. 4:12a NKJ). According to Ephesians 6:14, truth is part of the armor that enables us to prevail against the schemes of the devil. The apostle Paul wrote:

> Therefore put on the full armor of God, so that when the day of evil comes, you may be able to stand your ground, and after you have done everything, to stand. Stand firm then with the belt of truth buckled around your waist…"
>
> —Eph. 6:13-14a NIV

"If you abide in My word,
then you are truly disciples
of Mine; and you shall
know the truth, and the truth
shall make you free."

—John 8:31b–32

Above all, taking the shield of faith with which
you will be able to quench all the fiery darts of the
wicked one.

—Eph. 6:16 NKJ

With the belt of truth regarding God's love for me
now securely around my waist, I stood firm instead of
falling. Because I now believed this truth wholeheartedly,
my shield of faith quenched this attack of the enemy
and rendered it powerless. When we embrace the great
truths of His word, our shield of faith will quench *every*
arrow set on fire and hurled at us by the evil one. Not
some, not most, but *all* his flaming missiles.

The armor God has provided for the believer makes
him undefeatable. It is the inheritance of every believer
that no weapon turned against him will succeed. As
the prophet Isaiah wrote, "But in that coming day, no
weapon turned against you will succeed... These benefits
are enjoyed by the servants of the Lord; their vindica-
tion will come from Me. I, the Lord, have spoken"
(Isa. 54:17 NLT). After listing trials of many different
sorts, the apostle Paul concluded, "Yet in all these things
we are more than conquerors through Him who loved
us" (Rom. 8:37 NKJ).

I experienced a great healing of my mind. "For God
has not given us a spirit of fear, but of power and of love
and of a sound mind" (2 Tim. 1:7 NKJV). Mighty forces
may overpower us, but if we will set our love upon the
Lord, He will overpower them. As the psalmist wrote:

Because he has set his love upon Me,
Therefore I will deliver him;
I will set him on high,
Because he has known My name.
He shall call upon Me, and I will answer him;
I will be with him in trouble;
I will deliver him and honor him.
With long life I will satisfy him,
And show him My salvation.

—Ps. 91:14–16 NKJV

The word translated "salvation" in the Bible includes the meaning of deliverance, protection, and healing. When God shows us His salvation, He shows us His delivering power. In the first chapter of the book of Exodus, we read how the children of Israel became enslaved to the Egyptians for 400 long years. Since Egypt was the most powerful nation on the earth at the time and would never release the Hebrew slaves voluntarily, there seemed to be no hope that the Israelites would ever be free. Yet, "is anything too difficult for the Lord?" (Gen. 18:14a). Absolutely not! He sent Moses to rescue them, and this man of faith brought such great calamities upon the Egyptians that they were compelled to let His people go.

Yet, a short time afterward, the Egyptians had a change of heart, and set out in pursuit of the children of Israel, to re-enslave them. When the Israelites saw the great army of chariots marching towards them, they were terrified. With mountains on one side, desert on the other side, and the Red Sea before them, there was no way of escape.

> But Moses said to the people, "Do not fear! Stand by and see the salvation of the Lord which He will accomplish for you today; for the Egyptians whom you have seen today, you will never see them again forever.
>
> —Exodus 14:13-14

In spite of the imminent danger, Moses boldly declared, "Do not fear! Stand by and see the salvation of the Lord." The Lord then instructed Moses to stretch out his rod over the sea and divide it, so that the Israelites could cross over on dry land. Moses obeyed, and the children of Israel went through the midst of the sea on dry land. The Egyptians followed in after them. At daybreak, when the children of Israel had reached the other side, God instructed Moses to stretch out his rod over the water once more, this time causing the waters to return to their normal place. When Moses did so, the waters came back together, overthrowing the enemy in the midst of the sea.

> Thus the Lord saved Israel that day from the hand of the Egyptians, and Israel saw the Egyptians dead on the seashore. And when Israel saw the great power which the Lord had used against the Egyptians, the people feared the Lord, and they believed in the Lord and in His servant Moses.
>
> —Exodus 14:30-31

When the children of Israel saw the great power the Lord had used to save them—for their enemies, the Egyptians, lay dead on the seashore—they stopped fearing man and began fearing God.

Is there a Red Sea in your life? Do you feel trapped and powerless before the demonic powers that want to keep you in bondage? Then do not fear. Stand by and see the salvation of the Lord. He is still the Great Bondage Breaker who will shatter the power of the oppressor, while bringing a mighty deliverance to His people.

Jesus declared His great mission while at the synagogue in Nazareth:

> The Spirit of the Lord is upon Me, because
> He anointed Me to preach the gospel to the poor.
> He has sent Me to proclaim release to the captives,
> And recovery of sight to the blind,
> To set free those who are downtrodden,
> To proclaim the favorable year of the Lord.
> —Luke 4:18-19

> And He began to say to them, "Today this Scripture has been fulfilled in your hearing."
> —Luke 4:21

After reading this passage in Isaiah, Jesus made the astonishing statement that He, Himself, was the fulfillment of this prophesy. He came to minister to the poor, to proclaim liberty to those in bondage, to bring freedom to those who are downtrodden. Throughout the gospels, we see this powerful ministry in action, as He delivered the demon-possessed, restored sight to the blind, and healed the lame, the deaf, and those with leprosy. Now I personally experienced the reality of His great mission to liberate those who were bound. Though I had been downtrodden as a result of my own folly, the contempt of others, and the lies I had been fooled into believing, He had made me free.

"A battered reed He will not break off, and a smoldering wick He will not put out" (Matt. 12:20a). At the time this was written, reeds were used to make a flute-like musical instrument, to be played by shepherds as they watched over their sheep. If a reed became damaged, it would no longer make a pleasant musical sound, so the shepherd would break it and throw it away. Jesus said, "I am the Good Shepherd; I know My sheep and My sheep know Me" (John 10:14 NIV). This passage from Isaiah 42, quoted in Matthew 12, tells us that the Messiah would be a different kind of shepherd. When He encounters a damaged reed–a person whose life is badly scarred–He will not break it and throw it away. On the contrary, He will be especially gentle with that reed. Though I had been as a battered reed that people might have considered worthless, Jesus dealt with me with special care, loving me, nourishing me, and bringing healing to my soul.

The Lord challenged the condemning thoughts still going through my mind. Believers have the promise, "If we confess our sins, He is faithful and righteous to forgive us our sins and to cleanse us from all unrighteousness" (1 John 1:9). Confessing and renouncing our sins brings God's mercy, for Proverbs 28:13 says, "He who conceals his sins does not prosper, but whoever confesses and renounces them finds mercy" (NIV). This I had done, and had put my faith in Jesus. According to Romans 8:1, "Therefore, there is now no condemnation for those who are in Christ Jesus" (NIV). There was no record of any of my sins in God's books. They would be looked for and not be found, for they were lost in God's ocean of forgetfulness. As Micah the prophet wrote:

> Who is a God like You, who pardons sin and forgives the transgression of the remnant of His inheritance? You do not stay angry forever but delight to show mercy. You will again have compassion on us; You will tread our sins underfoot and hurl all our iniquities into the depths of the sea.
>
> —Micah 7:18-19 NIV

Therefore, I was cleared of all charges and declared justified before the Lord. It were just as though I had never sinned. John Stott explains that the word "justified" means "to be declared righteous, to be accepted, to stand in His favor, and under His smile" (*Only One Way: The Message of Galatians*, page 77).[4] It is the exact opposite of condemnation. Paul asks, "Who shall bring a charge against God's elect? It is God who justifies. Who is he who condemns?" (Rom. 8:33-34a NKJV).

The sorrow I'd experienced over the wrongs I had committed against Stephen had been a worldly sorrow. "For the sorrow that is according to the will of God produces a repentance without regret, leading to salvation; but the sorrow of the world produces death" (2 Cor. 7:10). Had it not produced a spiritual death, when I had said to myself, "I deserve to die. I'm such a rotten person"? Condemnation is from the devil, not God. Condemnation differs from conviction in that even if you repent, you won't feel any better. It's just one of the tools the devil uses to rob, kill and destroy. Condemnation robs a believer of his faith in the righteousness that Jesus paid such a high price to give him. If severely condemned, a person can become unable to believe that he is loved and valued by God. This was the main reason my deliverance had been so slow in coming. I disliked myself so much, I was unable to believe that God loved me as deeply as He does.

God sent Jesus into the world to bring life and salvation, not condemnation and death. "For God did not send His Son into the world to condemn the world, but to save the world through Him. Whoever believes in Him is not condemned, but whoever does not believe stands condemned already, because he has not believed in the name of God's one and only Son" (John 3:17-18 NIV). In the Amplified Version, verse 17 reads:

> "For God did not send the Son into the world in order to judge (to reject, to condemn, to pass sentence

on) the world, but that the world might find salvation and be made safe and sound through Him."
—John 3:17 Amp.

In other words, His mission was not to bring condemnation, but to remove it. I felt a tremendous lift as God's word made me free. "His choice is based on His grace, not on what they [people] have done. For if God's choice were based on what people do, then His grace would not be real grace" (Rom. 11:6, Good News Version). This is the whole meaning of His mercy. It meant that my mistakes had not been final. It meant that His mercy and power were greater than my mistakes. If a person sees either his own mistakes or those of another as final, it is because he does not know the Redeemer; he does not know the One who can cause old things to pass away and make all things new. He does not know the One who gave His life to justify the ungodly. God is merciful to the person who confesses and renounces his sin. But he who doesn't think such mercy should exist will never obtain it. "For judgment will be merciless to one who has shown no mercy; mercy triumphs over judgment" (James 2:13). Jesus taught in His great Sermon on the Mount that, "Blessed are the merciful, for they shall receive mercy" (Matt. 5:7). The word translated "they" in this verse has the meaning "they and only they." So this verse could be rendered,

"Blessed are the merciful, for they and only they shall receive mercy."

I learned from Scripture that God is my Judge, not man. Jesus declared, "Judge not that you be not judged" (Matt. 7:1 NKJ). Of course, that doesn't mean we are not to evaluate other people at all, for several verses later, Jesus tells us not to give what is holy to dogs, nor cast our pearls before swine. In order to determine who are "dogs" and "swine," we must exercise judgment.

Yet Scripture forbids setting ourselves up as someone else's judge, for in doing so, we put ourselves in God's place. No one is accountable to *us* for everything they do. *God* is their Judge, not us. Romans 14:12-13a says, "So then, each of us will give an account of himself to God. Therefore, let us stop passing judgment on one another." (NIV) If we are foolish enough to make judgments only God has the right to make, He will judge *us*.

The apostle Paul admonished believers in Corinth not to judge one another, saying, "Therefore do not go on passing judgment before the time, but wait until the Lord comes, who will both bring to light the things hidden in the darkness and disclose the motives of men's hearts; and then each man's praise will come to him from God" (1 Cor. 4:5). I discovered that God judges people differently from the way we tend to judge each other, "for God sees not as man sees, for man looks at the outward appearance, but the Lord looks at the heart" (1 Samuel 16:7b). These passages make it clear that it is foolish to judge another, that only God knows the true intents of the heart, that from only Him is nothing hidden.

After all, who are we to judge someone else? Jesus challenged those who wanted to stone a woman caught in adultery, saying, "He who is without sin among you, let him be the first to throw a stone at her" (John 8:7b).

The apostle Paul wrote, "But with me it is a very small thing that I should be judged by you...but He who judges me is the Lord" (1 Cor. 4:3a, 4b NKJV). To be judged by another is a *small* thing. I'd been treating it like a *big* thing. But really, it held no weight. It had no authority. Other people are not my judge. Paul asks the believers in Rome, "Who are you to judge someone else's servant? To his own master he stands or falls. And he will stand, for the Lord is able to make him stand" (Rom. 14:4 NIV). From these Scriptures, I realized, *I will stand or fall before my own Master, and I will stand, because the Lord is able to make me stand!* Yes, I realized that I didn't need to be afraid of anyone. "If God is for us, who can be against us?" (Rom. 8:31 NKJV). As David wrote:

> The Lord is my light and my salvation;
> Whom shall I fear?
> The Lord is the strength of my life;
> Of whom shall I be afraid?
>
> —Psalm 27:1 NKJ

Solomon wrote,

> The fear of man brings a snare, but he who trusts in
> the Lord will be exalted.
>
> —Prov. 29:25

My fear that others would reject me had been an
enormous snare, creating an escalating cycle of fear, rejection, more fear, and more rejection. Both Saul and David
discovered what a snare the fear of man can be. Saul,
Israel's first king, was a man who lived in fear. His fear
of people caused him to disobey the Lord. Therefore, the
Lord declared to him through the prophet Samuel:

> "Because you have rejected the word of the Lord, He
> has rejected you as king." Then Saul said to Samuel,
> "I have sinned. I violated the Lord's command and
> your instructions. I was afraid of the people and so
> I gave in to them."
>
> —1 Sam. 15:23b-24 NIV

Saul's fear of man resulted in action that was contrary to the will of God. Like Saul, my fear of man caused
me to miss the mark. To take Saul's place, God chose
a man after His own heart–David. Soon afterward, the
Philistines, led by their champion Goliath, threatened
the armies of Israel. Now the Philistines were much more
powerful than the Israelites. They alone had weapons
of iron, which gave them a huge advantage over Israel.

Yet God had promised His people that if they would diligently obey the Lord, "The Lord will cause your enemies who rise up against you to be defeated before you; they shall come out against you one way and shall flee before you seven ways" (Deut. 28:7). How did Saul respond? 1 Samuel 17:11 tells us, "When Saul and all Israel heard these words of the Philistine [Goliath], they were dismayed and greatly afraid." Saul was terrified when he heard Goliath's threats. Instead of believing that God was more than able to give them the victory, he shook with fear. This in turn caused the whole army to lose heart. Because of his fear, he made no attempt to drive the enemy back, but instead, was intimidated by their threats. Likewise, my fear made me powerless against my spiritual enemies, who were able to badger and intimidate me at will.

But David knew how to trust God. To Goliath, David declared:

> You come against me with sword and spear and javelin, but I come against you in the name of the Lord Almighty, the God of the armies of Israel, whom you have defied.
>
> —1 Samuel 17:45 NIV

Confident that God would give Israel the victory, David continued:

All those gathered here will know that it is not by sword or spear that the Lord saves; for the battle is the Lord's, and He will give all of you into our hands.

—1 Samuel 17:47 NIV

David then took a stone in his sling and aimed it at the giant's forehead. He hit his target with perfect accuracy. Goliath fell to the ground, dead. To celebrate this great victory, the women came out of all the towns dancing. Scripture says:

As they danced, they sang, "Saul has slain his thousands, and David his tens of thousands." Saul was very angry; this refrain galled him. "They have credited David with tens of thousands," he thought, "but me with only thousands. What more can he get but the kingdom?" And from that time on Saul kept a jealous eye on David.

—1 Samuel 18:7-9 NIV

After the women sang higher praises of David than of Saul, Saul became very jealous of David. But he was also afraid of his rival. Three times throughout 1 Samuel 18, we read of Saul's fear of David, a fear that kept increasing:

Saul was afraid of David, because the Lord was with David but had left Saul.

—1 Sam. 18:12 NIV

When Saul saw how successful he [David] was, he was afraid of him.

—1 Sam. 18:15 NIV

> When Saul realized that the Lord was with David and
> that his daughter Michal loved David, Saul became
> still more afraid of him, and he remained his enemy
> the rest of his days.
>
> —1 Sam. 18:28 NIV

Fear of David caused Saul to become David's enemy. Had not my fear of Stephen done the same? Saul wasn't content to sit at home filled with envy and fear. He set out to kill the king-to-be, attempting if possible, to thwart the very purposes of God. As David played his harp for the king one day, as was his custom, Saul threw his spear at him, hoping to pin him to the wall. David fled to his house. But Saul wasn't about to give up. We read in 1 Sam. 19:

> Saul sent men to David's house to watch it and to
> kill him in the morning. But Michal, David's wife,
> warned him, "If you don't run for your life tonight,
> tomorrow you'll be killed." So Michal let David
> down through a window, and he fled and escaped.
>
> —1 Sam. 19:11-12 NIV

During this trial, he wrote Psalm 59. First, he cries out to the Lord for protection from these evil men and appeals to the Lord, saying he has done no wrong. Yet his closing words are words of victory and praise:

> But I will sing of Your strength, in the morning I
> will sing of Your love; for You are my Fortress, my
> Refuge in times of trouble. O my Strength, I sing

praise to You; You, O God, are my Fortress, my loving God.

—Ps. 59:16-17 NIV

God honoured his faith by making Saul and those he sent after David, powerless to lay a hand on him (See 1 Sam. 19:19-24).

Yet only a short time later, David, too, became fearful. Now, instead of speaking words of faith, he says to Saul's son, Jonathan, "Yet as surely as the Lord lives and as you live, there is only a step between me and death" (1 Sam. 20:3b NIV). Terrified, he fled to Nob, the city of the priests. Here, he deceived the priest regarding why he had come, requested food, and asked for either a sword or spear. Since Goliath's sword was being stored here, wrapped in a cloth behind the ephod, the priest gave it to David.

From there he fled to Achish, king of Gath, the very hometown of Goliath! There the king's men recognized him immediately, saying, "Isn't this David, the king of the land? Isn't he the one they sing about in their dances: 'Saul has slain his thousands and David his tens of thousands?'" (1 Sam. 21:11 NIV) Notice David's response in the next verse:

> David took these words to heart and **was very much afraid of Achish king of Gath.** So he pretended to be insane in their presence; and while he was in their hands, he acted like a madman, making marks on the doors of the gate and letting saliva run down his beard.
>
> —1 Sam. 21:12-13 NIV

Fearful the king would order his execution, he pretended to be insane, scribbling on the doors of the city gate and letting his saliva run down his beard. The tactic worked: Achish promptly drove him out of town.

Yet from this experience, he wrote Psalm 34, in which he once again put his feet upon the Rock. First he praises and magnifies the Lord. Then he declares:

> I sought the Lord, and He heard me,
> And delivered me from all my fears.
> —Psalm 34:4 NKJ

What had God delivered him from? From his enemies? God had done this, certainly. But notice what David says in verse 4. Here David rejoices because God had delivered him from all his *fears!* Fear had caused him to lie and to arm himself with Goliath's sword, in spite of having declared earlier, "It is not by sword or spear that the Lord saves, for the battle is the Lord's" (1 Sam. 17:47 NIV). In fact, Goliath's sword had failed to protect even Goliath! His fears had compelled him to do what was not logical: to take refuge in Gath, the very hometown of Goliath. His fears had taken him into the enemy's camp, the very enemy over whom he had previously won such a stunning victory. This action increased the risk of his being killed, not decreased it, as intended. Fear caused him to draw back from trusting God, to put his trust in the arm of flesh, and to make a fool out of himself. Had he remained strong in faith, he would

"I sought the Lord,
and He heard me,
and delivered me from
all my fears."
— Psalm 34:4 NKJ

have remained untouchable by Saul, and would never have given his enemies, the Philistines, the opportunity to seize him and hold him in custody.

Likewise, when I allowed fear to dominate my life, I armed myself with a death wish that I didn't need and that couldn't protect me. Fear had led to irrational, self-defeating acts and had taken me straight into enemy territory. Fear enabled the devil and his legion of helpers to hold me as their prisoner.

Because I had placed my trust in man, a curse had been upon my life, for Jeremiah wrote, "Cursed is the one who trusts in man, who depends on flesh for his strength" (Jer. 17:5a NIV). The prophet goes on to describe this man, saying, "He will be like a bush in the wastelands … He will dwell in the parched places of the desert, in a salt land where no one lives" (Jer. 17:6 NIV). Looking in the wrong place for the fulfillment of my emotional needs had created a wasteland in my life. I had been like a bush trying to grow in a salty desert where nothing could grow and nothing could live. It had alienated people from my life and caused me to become more and more needy.

But now that I trusted in God, now that I lived to please Him, a transformation had occurred:

> But blessed is the man who trusts in the Lord,
> Whose confidence is in Him.
> He will be like a tree planted by the water
> That sends out its roots by the stream.
> It does not fear when heat comes;
> Its leaves are always green.

It has no worries in a year of drought
And never fails to bear fruit.

—Jeremiah 17:7-8 NIV

Notice how a person whose trust is in God enjoys freedom from fear. No matter what goes wrong, he is not anxious. The Lord gives him great peace, for his mind is fixed on God.

Though it seemed as though I were stumbling over Victoria, my trial had actually brought to an end my life without God. From these difficulties, I saw my need for the Lord, for mercy, and for salvation. Never again could I say that love did not exist, for I had seen God's love shatter and defeat the power that Satan had over me. Never again could I live just for myself. Now, aware of my true purpose, the whole direction of my life changed.

The stronger my relationship with the Lord became, the more my relationships with other people improved. The longer I walked with the Lord, the more I acquired His wisdom. My wisdom had been folly, "but the wisdom that is from above is first pure, then peaceable, gentle, willing to yield, full of mercy and good fruits, without partiality and without hypocrisy" (James 3:17 NKJV). I realized that it is a great thing to love those who do not love me. For Jesus taught:

> Love your enemies, do good to those who hate you, bless those who curse you, pray for those who mistreat you.
>
> —Luke 6:27-28

God not only loves us with an everlasting love, He has commanded us to love others, even our enemies. We are to seek the highest good of others, whether they love us or not. Those who hate us, we are to help. Those who curse us, we are to bless. Those who mistreat us, we are to pray for.

I discovered a height, depth, and breadth of love unknown to me before my conversion. Nothing the world can offer, no matter how mighty or spectacular, can match the vastness of this love, which is eternal and unending. Before my conversion, it was impossible for me to truly love other people. I had not received the love that would enable me to give it away. Now I was becoming a blessing to other people, instead of a curse and a stumbling block, for "the one who loves his brother abides in the light and there is no cause for stumbling in him" (1 John 2:10).

Surely, it is a lack of love that leads to these crippling fears of rejection. As John writes, "There is no fear in love, but perfect love casts out fear" (1 John 4:18a). Paul describes this love in his letter to the Corinthian believers:

Love is patient, love is kind, and is not jealous;
love does not brag and is not arrogant, does not act
unbecomingly; it does not seek its own, is not provoked, does not take into account a wrong suffered,
does not rejoice in unrighteousness, but rejoices
with the truth; [Love] bears all things, believes all
things, hopes all things, endures all things. Love
never fails.

—1 Cor. 13:4-8a

Paul writes at the beginning of the next chapter,
"Eagerly pursue and seek to acquire [this] love [make
it your aim, your great quest]…" (1 Cor. 14:1a Amplified Bible).

Without love, we are nothing:

And if I have the gift of prophecy, and know all
mysteries and all knowledge; and if I have all faith,
so as to remove mountains, but do not have love,
I am nothing.

—1 Cor. 13:2, italics added

With it, we will never fail, because love never fails!
Have you done terrible things? Do you think
you will never count for much in God's eyes? Hear
what Jesus explained to Simon, the Pharisee, who
looked with distain on a repentant prostitute who loved
Jesus:

And Jesus answered and said to him, "Simon, I have
something to say to you." And he replied, "Say it,

Teacher." "A certain moneylender had two debtors: one owed five hundred denarii, and the other fifty. When they were unable to repay, he graciously forgave them both. Which of them therefore will love him more?" Simon answered and said, "I suppose the one whom he forgave more." And He said to him, "You have judged correctly."

—Luke 7:40-43

Then the Lord explained to Simon that he had failed to show Jesus even the customary kindness normally shown to a guest. Yet this woman hadn't stopped expressing her love for Him from the moment He had come in.

"For this reason I say to you, her sins, which are many, have been forgiven, for she loved much; but he who is forgiven little, loves little."

—Luke 7:47

If you have committed many sins or very serious sins, then according to Jesus, you will love Him far more than someone who has been forgiven much less. That's encouraging news! We see this with the apostle Paul. He viciously persecuted believers in an attempt to stamp out Christianity. But after a powerful encounter with Jesus on his way to Damascus (see Acts 9), he became a believer. He went on to become the greatest apostle, founding churches throughout the Roman Empire and writing a substantial portion of the New Testament. He writes to Timothy:

> This is a true saying, and everyone should believe it: Christ Jesus came into the world to save sinners – and I was the worst of them all. But that is why God had mercy on me, so that Christ Jesus could use me as a prime example of His great patience with even the worst sinners. Then others will realize that they, too, can believe in Him and receive eternal life.
>
> —1 Tim. 1:15-16 NLT

Has your sin made you an outcast? Consider Matthew. He was a tax collector, one of the most despised groups in Jewish society. Tax collectors collected revenue for the Roman government, but often lined their own pockets at the same time. They were known for their greed, dishonesty, and extortion. They became very, very wealthy at the expense of their own people, who regarded them as traitors. They were not allowed in the synagogues, nor were they permitted to have any social contact with other Jews. They were ranked with unclean animals. They were regarded as no better than pigs, robbers, pimps, and murderers.

Though all tax collectors were despised by other Jews, toll collectors were the most despised of all. These officials collected tolls, tariffs, customs, and other such taxes. As there was more room for fraud when collecting these types of taxes, toll collectors were especially

"There is no fear in
love; but perfect love
casts out fear."
　　　　　—1 John 4:18a

dishonest and oppressive. Guess what? Matthew was a toll collector. Yet Jesus chose *him* to be one of the twelve apostles whom He sent throughout Galilee to do mighty exploits in His name (see Luke 9:1-2). Jesus chose *him* to turn the world upside down by proclaiming the gospel far and wide after the resurrection. To him was given the noble task of writing the gospel of Matthew! And finally, Jesus appointed *him,* along with the other apostles, to one day sit on twelve thrones, judging the twelve tribes of Israel. One of the greatest of sinners became one of the greatest of men.

Do others shun you? Consider the people Jesus ministered to in Matthew 8. The first was a man stricken with leprosy, the most dreaded disease in the ancient world. No other medical condition brought such ostracism and reproach. Because leprosy was highly contagious, and because touching a leper made a person ceremonially unclean, a leper was forced to live outside the city. Everywhere he went, he had to cry out, "Unclean! Unclean!" No one would touch him or even come near him. Many rabbis would throw stones at a leper to drive him away. So this man would have *fled* from a rabbi. Yet he came to Jesus, saying, "Lord, if You are willing, you can make me clean" (Matt. 8:2b).

This afflicted man knew Jesus *could* heal him, but was uncertain whether He *would*. So Jesus assured him that He *was* willing:

And He stretched out His hand and touched him, saying, "I am willing; be cleansed." And immediately his leprosy was cleansed.

—Matt. 8:3

Jesus touched him! It may have been a long, long time since he had felt the touch of another person. How his heart must have longed for a caring touch! Jesus could have healed him with a word, "Be healed." But He didn't shun or avoid this unfortunate man, whose heart must have been broken. Instead, "He stretched out His hand and *touched* him!"

Are you broken-hearted over things that have happened in your life? Are you wondering if God is willing to heal your broken heart? God is willing! Jesus wants to touch you! Just come to Him in simple faith and He will receive you.

Yes, lepers were despised. But there were others. Many Jewish men thanked God everyday that they had not been born a Gentile, a slave, or a woman. Women were regarded as little more than property. And Jewish people would not even eat a meal with a Gentile. Yet as we continue to read in Matthew 8, we find that these were the very people Jesus ministered to. Here, Jesus heals Peter's mother-in-law, and shows mercy to a Gentile centurion by healing his slave. So no matter how many may reject you, if you believe on Him, God will embrace you.

How secure are we in God's love? Will anything ever separate us from His love? After naming trials of various kinds, Paul writes:

> Yet in all these things we are more than conquerors through Him who loved us. For I am persuaded that neither death nor life, nor angels nor principalities nor powers, nor things present nor things to come, nor height nor depth, nor any other created thing, shall be able to separate us from the love of God which is in Christ Jesus our Lord.
>
> —Romans 8:37-39 NKJ

CHAPTER 9

pressing on

"He must increase, but I must decrease."

—John 3:30

I am learning how vital it is to be armed with a comprehensive knowledge of God's word, to know its authority, and to stand on it without wavering. I'm realizing that the more His word is engraved upon my heart, the more power and victory I will have. There's no shortage of power from God's end. The very power that raised Christ from the dead works on our behalf! Paul prayed that God would give the believers at Ephesus a revelation of this, saying,

> I pray that the eyes of your heart may be enlightened,
> so that you may know what is the hope of His calling,

what are the riches of the glory of His inheritance in the saints, and what is the surpassing greatness of His power toward us who believe. These are in accordance with the working of the strength of His might which He brought about in Christ, when He raised Him from the dead, and seated Him at His right hand in the heavenly places..."

—Eph. 1:18-20

With that degree of power working to free us from everything outside of God's will, not a believer in the world should live in bondage and defeat.

God has already defeated the devil and all his cohorts. He has already risen from the dead in complete triumph over them. Paul writes, "When He had disarmed the rulers and authorities, He made a public display of them, having triumphed over them through Him" (Col. 2:15). In ancient times, when one nation defeated another, those on the losing side would be paraded in chains down the streets of the victors, so all could see their disgrace and defeat. This was the very humiliation the Lord Jesus compelled the powers of darkness to endure when He rose from the dead. He made an open parade of their defeat before all the angels in glory. His victory is our victory, for we were identified with Him both in His death and in His resurrection. The old me was crucified with Christ and put to death. The new me was raised up together with Him and is now seated with Him in heavenly places at the right hand of God.

What's the result? Believers are now dead to sin and alive to God, for Romans 6:11 says, "Even so consider yourselves to be dead to sin, but alive to God in Christ Jesus." We are seated far above the sphere where the kingdom of darkness resides. The devil and all his host of demons are under our feet! We don't need to strain to become victorious, for God has already won for us every victory we will ever need in this life. The apostle Paul writes, "Thanks be to God, who gives us the victory through our Lord Jesus Christ" (1 Cor. 15:57).

God has given me victory over fear, feeling unloved, and being an approval addict. He has also given me victory over lupus. I have now been in remission for over 20 years. After ten years, recovery is considered permanent. To God be all the praise!

God has not withheld even the very best, His Son, from us. Will He not also give us the lesser things? Paul wrote, "He who did not spare His own Son, but delivered Him up for us all, how will He not also with Him freely give us all things?" (Rom 8:32) God has freely given us *all things!* We will possess them when we take hold of them with our faith.

One Christian author explains that the kingdom of God is like a game of checkers. God makes the first move by giving us His promise. Then the next move is ours. He will not move again until we move. We take our turn when we take hold of what God has promised with our faith and believe that it is already ours. This

"Thanks be to God who gives us the victory through our Lord Jesus Christ."

—1 Cor. 15:57

involves thanking Him for it each day by faith, before we see the manifestation. Then the next move is God's. He responds to our faith by bringing to pass what we have been believing for.

Because He is a great God and the author and finisher of my faith, the work He has begun will be brought to completion. Paul wrote, "For I am confident of this very thing, that He who began a good work in you will perfect it until the day of Christ Jesus" (Phil. 1:6). But He needs my cooperation. One of the ways I cooperate with God, is to live to please Him, not man. It not only lets Him get the job done, but it keeps me from being in bondage to the approval of others.

Our worth has nothing to do with the opinion others have of us. We shouldn't be concerned with what others think of us. Instead, being faithful to God and doing His will should be our supreme goal and desire. Then we will hear Him say to us, "Well done, good and faithful servant! You have been faithful with a few things; I will put you in charge of many things. Come and share your master's happiness!" (Matt. 25:21 NIV)

Without Him, I can do absolutely nothing, for Jesus told His disciples, "I am the vine; you are the branches. If a man remains in Me and I in him, he will bear much fruit; apart from Me you can do nothing" (John 15:5 NIV). But as long as I remain in Him and He in I, He has promised that I will bear much fruit. His enabling power is unlimited, for Paul wrote, "I can do all things through Christ who strengthens me" (Phil. 4:13 NKJ).

I am a witness to His power. Though I was filled with darkness, He has made me a light of the world.

As I am faithful to tell of the great things He has done for me, I am strengthened further. Scripture declares, "They overcame him [the devil] because of the blood of the Lamb and because of the word of their testimony" (Rev. 12:11a).

My entire composing experience has changed. His word has become my inspiration and His glory, the goal. Gone are the cycles of sweeping highs and devastating lows, the struggles, the exasperations. Emotional problems no longer cripple me. I no longer try to prove that I have a worth I do not believe I have. A firm foundation of self-worth and victory is my starting point, and all my creative endeavors are the fruit of that foundation.

My victory has not been a victory over anyone. I have not won by proving my case or winning a point. My victory has been a gradual descending of self from the throne of my life and an invitation to the Lord to ascend in my place as King and Ruler. I did not win by my own defenses. I won when the Lord became my defense. With His love and power, He disarmed me of my own means of protection and rearmed me with an armor that will never fail.

Prayer to Receive Jesus As Your Savior

If you do not know Jesus as your Lord and Savior and would like to give your life to Him now, pray the following prayer:

> Dear Lord Jesus, I admit that I am a sinner, and have sinned repeatedly all my life. I know I deserve to spend eternity in unspeakable torment. I'm so grateful You died to pay the penalty for all my sins. Come into my heart. Become my Lord and Savior. Wash away my sins. Make me a new person.

endnote

1   C.S. Lewis, *Mere Christianity,* (New York: The Mac-Millan Company, 1960), pages 40-41.

2   Dr. Herbert Shelton, *The Hygienic System, Vol. 2 Orthotrophy* (San Antonio, Texas, Published by Dr. Shelton's Health School; First edition, 1935); page 474.

3. John Stott, *Only One Way: The Message of Galatians* (London, England; Inter-Varsity Press, 1968), page 77.

4. Maurice Rawlings, M.D., *Beyond Death's Door: The Life After Life Bestseller* (New York City, New York, Bantam Books, 1978).

Disclaimer

The information provided in this book in no way constitutes medical advice for any specific medical conditions or individuals who may read this book. For medical advice, consult your physician.

forgiveness video

By Beverley Brown

Have you been struggling with resentment or bitterness toward someone who has wronged you?

In this helpful teaching by Beverley Brown, you will learn that:

- if you do not forgive, God will not forgive you.
- unforgiveness gives the devil ground in your life, allowing him to interfere in your life in ways you may not have suspected.
- how praying for the offender and trusting God to be your avenger and vindicator can help you overcome unforgiveness.

View this entire video online at <u>bevbrownministries.com</u> and allow God's word to liberate you from any bitterness that may be in your heart.

Printed in the United States
122521LV00001B/82-114/P

9 781414 107363